Sacagawea

Sacagawea

Stacy DeKeyser

Franklin Watts
A Division of Scholastic Inc.
New York • Toronto • London • Auckland • Sydney
Mexico City • New Delhi • Hong Kong
Danbury, Connecticut

For Tom and Steven, and especially for Kelly

Note to readers: Definitions for words in **bold** can be found in the Glossary at the back of this book.

Photographs © 2004: Art Resource, NY/National Portrait Gallery, Smithsonian Institution, Washington DC, U.S.A: 49 bottom; Bridgeman Art Library International Ltd., London/New York: 11 (Musee Franco-Americaine, Blerancourt, Chauny, France), 46 (New-York Historical Society, New York, USA), 13, 33 (Private Collection), 25 (Royal Geographical Society, London, UK); Clymer Museum of Art, reproduced with permission of Mrs. John F. Clymer: 50 (Down the South Platte, Baptiste Charbonneau, by John F. Clymer), 32 (Lewis and Clark in the Bitteroots, by John F. Clymer), 37 (Sacajawea at the Big Water, by John F. Clymer), 44 (Up the Jefferson, by John F. Clymer); Corbis Images/Annie Griffiths Belt: 41; Gary R. Lucy Gallery Inc., Washington, Missouri: 21 (Lewis and Clark: The Departure from the Wood River Encampment, May14, 1804, by Gary R. Lucy); Michael Haynes: 5, 6, 17, 18; Montana Historical Society, Helena/Henry Lion: 42; Nativestock.com/Marilynn "Angel" Wynn: 2, 9, 19, 24, 27, 29, 52; North Wind Picture Archives: 14, 15, 22, 23, 38; Ron Sanders: 5, 35; South Dakota State Historical Society, State Archives: 49 top; Stock Montage, Inc.: 8, 51; The Image Works/Sonda Dawes: 30, 31.

Cover illustration by Stephen Marchesi.

Map by XNR Productions, Inc.

The illustration on the cover shows Sacagawea. The photograph opposite the title page shows the Lemhi Pass in what is now Idaho, one of the many places Sacagawea and the Lewis and Clark expedition passed through on their travels.

Library of Congress Cataloging-in-Publication Data

DeKeyser, Stacy.
    Sacagawea / by Stacy DeKeyser.
        p. cm. — (Watts library)
    Summary: A biography of the Shoshoni woman who served on the Lewis and Clark Expedition as a guide and interpreter.
    ISBN 0-531-12290-5 (lib. bdg.)   0-531-16385-7 (pbk.)
    Includes bibliographical references and index.
    1. Sacagawea—Juvenile literature. 2. Shoshoni women—Biography—Juvenile literature. 3. Shoshoni Indians—Biography—Juvenile literature. 4. Lewis and Clark Expedition (1804–1806)—Juvenile literature. [1. Sacagawea. 2. Shoshoni Indians—Biography. 5. Lewis and Clark Expedition (1804–1806)] I. Title. II. Series.
F592.7.S123D45 2004
978.004'974574'0092—dc22
                                              2003013342

Contents

Since Sacagawea lived before the age of photography, artists have tried to imagine what she may have looked like. This recent sketch shows her with her son.

Chapter One

In the Year 1801

In 1801, a young Shoshone girl was torn from her family and began a new life on the North American plains. In that same year, many hundreds of miles away, the United States swore in a new president. The president was one of the most respected men in the country. He lived in a mansion in Washington, D.C. The girl was a captive of strangers, and she lived on the plains beyond the boundaries of the United States. Although they never met, this young girl helped the president achieve one of his greatest dreams. She helped pave the way for the United States to become a large and powerful nation. The president's name was Thomas Jefferson. The Shoshone girl's name was Sacagawea.

A View from the East

In 1801, Thomas Jefferson became president of the United States. The country had grown since 1776, when Jefferson had written the Declaration of Independence. Now its states and

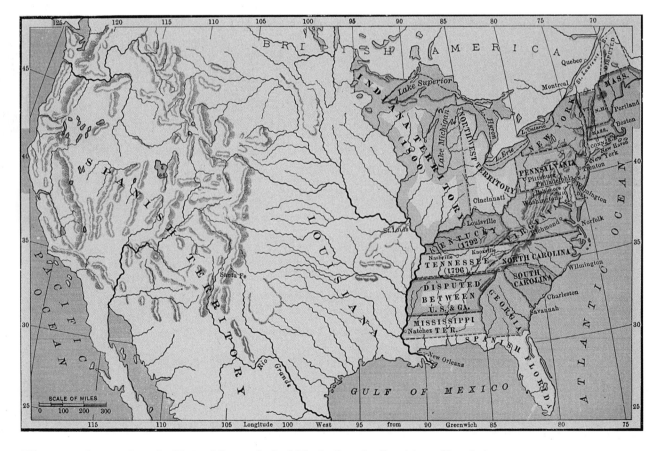

This map shows what the United States looked like before the Louisiana Purchase.

8

territories reached all the way to the Mississippi River. President Jefferson had a grand **ambition**, however. He hoped that someday the United States would reach even farther—all the way to the Pacific Ocean.

The United States was not a crowded place. In 1801, nine out of every ten U.S. citizens still lived near the Atlantic coast. Only four roads crossed the Appalachian Mountains. The territory between the Appalachians and the Mississippi River was still wild and sparsely settled.

The western lands were not just there for the taking, either. Louisiana—the huge territory that stretched from the Mississippi River to the Rocky Mountains—belonged to France.

Thomas Jefferson believed that buying the West would help the United States become a more powerful country.

9

Several countries hoped to lay claim to the land west of the Rocky Mountains to the Pacific Ocean, including Spain, Great Britain, and Russia.

Lots of people already lived beyond the U.S. frontier. Many thousands of American Indians, making up many different nations, were settled across the continent. They had been living there for centuries.

Thomas Jefferson wanted to learn about the American Indians, about the land, and about its resources. He also wanted the United States to be a powerful nation. To achieve that goal, Jefferson wanted the lands beyond the Mississippi River to belong to the United States.

The Unknown West

Jefferson had only a vague idea of what lay beyond the Mississippi River. Explorers and trappers had ventured westward from the United States and from Canada. They had described some of the American Indian peoples and talked about a rich supply of furs. A few European and American ships had explored the Pacific coast and the mouth of the Columbia River. The deepest interior of North America was still a mystery, however.

Jefferson wanted to find out. He had spent years learning everything he could about the American West. He had read that the Rocky Mountains were small and easy to cross compared with the rugged Appalachian Mountains. Most of all, Jefferson wanted to find the Northwest Passage, a waterway

crossing the western mountains that people at that time believed would link the Mississippi and Missouri Rivers with the Columbia River and the Pacific Ocean.

In 1801, there were no railroads, no airplanes, and no cars. Most roads were just dirt paths. The fastest way to transport mail, supplies, and people was by boat. Jefferson knew that if the United States could control the rivers of North America, it could control trade throughout the whole continent. Jefferson decided that he would try to buy Louisiana's most important city, New Orleans, from France. The United States would then control trade on the Mississippi River. After that, he would send a team of explorers all the way to the Pacific to

The French and U.S. flags fly over New Orleans just before the United States takes control of the Louisiana Territory.

11

find the Northwest Passage. The United States would then control all trade in the West. The United States would indeed become one of the most powerful countries in the world.

Despite his studies, Jefferson knew that the West had many unknowns. He would give his explorers strict instructions to write down everything they could about their experiences. He would ask them to collect samples of newly discovered plants and animals, to make detailed maps, and to describe the American Indian tribes they met. The expedition would be not only a way to explore the land bought by the United States, but it would also be a scientific expedition.

A View from the West

The American Indians who lived in the West had learned to forge an existence over many generations. Winters were harsh, and summers were hot and dry. Food could be hard to find. Only a few tribes had horses, and even fewer had guns for hunting or protection. A tribe had to be stronger than other tribes, or it would eventually be wiped out. Wars between tribes were common.

Around 1800, at about the time Thomas Jefferson became president, one of these small wars was taking place on the vast, unknown plains. A group of Shoshone (or Snake) Indians was hunting buffalo. Far from their home in the shelter of the Rocky Mountains in what is now Idaho, they were raided by another tribe, the Hidatsa (or Minnetarees). Some of the Shoshone escaped on their horses. Some were killed in the

Horses

Horses are not **native** to North America. They were brought by Spanish explorers in the 1500s.

raid. Others were taken captive, including a young girl about eleven years old. She was taken to live in a Hidatsa village on the banks of the Missouri River in what is now North Dakota. This young girl was given a new name: Sacagawea, meaning "Bird Woman."

The Shoshone had traveled from the Rocky Mountains to hunt buffalo when they were raided by another Indian group.

This engraving shows what a Mandan Indian village looked like in the early 1800s.

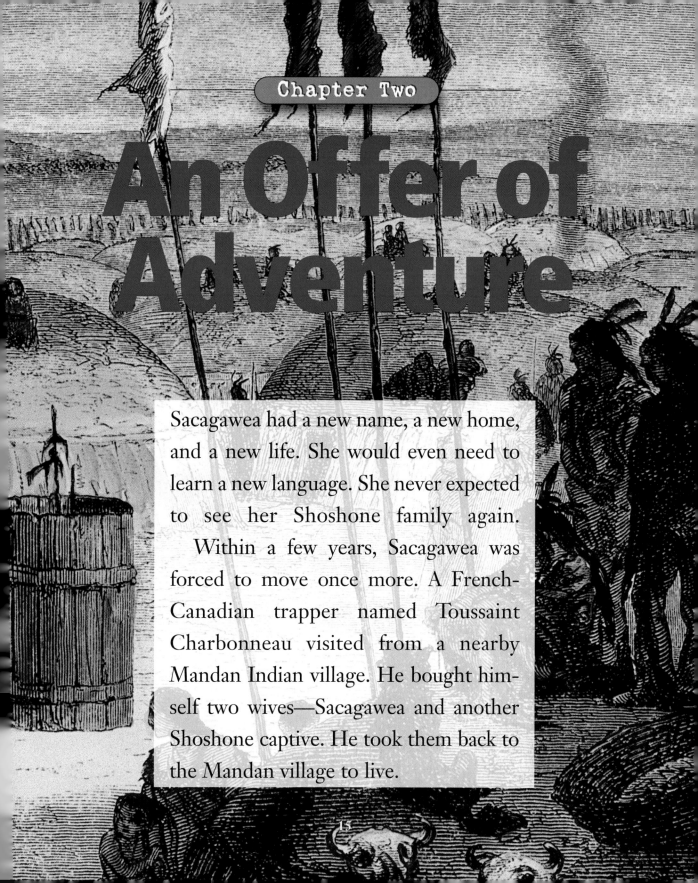

Chapter Two

An Offer of Adventure

Sacagawea had a new name, a new home, and a new life. She would even need to learn a new language. She never expected to see her Shoshone family again.

Within a few years, Sacagawea was forced to move once more. A French-Canadian trapper named Toussaint Charbonneau visited from a nearby Mandan Indian village. He bought himself two wives—Sacagawea and another Shoshone captive. He took them back to the Mandan village to live.

A Twist of Fate

In November of 1804, when Sacagawea was about sixteen years old, a troop of white men built a fort near the Mandan village. They were U.S. Army soldiers, led by two captains: Meriwether Lewis and William Clark. These were the explorers Thomas Jefferson had sent to find the Northwest Passage. The president had succeeded in buying not just New Orleans, but all of the Louisiana territory. The United States was now double in size and extended all the way to the Rocky Mountains.

The explorers, who were called the **Corps** of Discovery by Congress, were making a winter camp. They spent the bitter winter months learning everything they could about the western lands from the Hidatsa and the Mandan. Lewis and Clark learned they would need interpreters to help them communicate with the many tribes of American Indians they would meet along their journey. They would also need horses to get across the Rocky Mountains. The Mandan and the Hidatsa told Lewis and Clark about a tribe at the foot of the Rockies that owned many horses. That tribe was the Shoshone, Sacagawea's people.

Lewis and Clark had to find someone who could speak Shoshone so that they could **negotiate** for horses. They found out about Charbonneau's two Shoshone wives and hired him for the expedition, even though he could not speak Shoshone or English. The captains told Charbonneau to bring one wife with him—Sacagawea. Charbonneau explained that she was

Our Little Secret

When Meriwether Lewis chose William Clark to help command the expedition, he asked President Jefferson to give Clark a captain's **commission**, but army officials turned him down. Clark was officially a lieutenant. Lewis and Clark never told their men, and as far as the Corps of Discovery was concerned, they had two captains, equal in command.

going to give birth soon, and they said she could bring the baby along. Sacagawea would be the only woman allowed to go.

Lewis and Clark talk with Charbonneau while Sacagawea looks on.

A Fine Boy

On February 11, 1805, Sacagawea was ready to have her baby. By evening, however, the baby still had not been born. René Jessaume, a French trader living with the Mandan people, suggested that crushed rattlesnake rattle would help speed up the birth. Not too sure of the truth in it, Captain Lewis decided that it couldn't hurt.

Lewis dug out a rattlesnake rattle he had been saving to send back to President Jefferson. He gave it to Jessaume, who

Sacagawea's son would grow up to become an adventurer in his own right.

broke off two rings of the rattle, crushed them, and mixed them with water. Sacagawea drank the mixture, and ten minutes later she gave birth to a boy. Lewis was impressed, but he was pretty sure it was just a **coincidence**. He dutifully recorded the event in his journal: "This evening one of the wives of Charbono was delivered of a fine boy." The baby was named Jean Baptiste Charbonneau. Captain Clark would come to call him Pomp.

Under Way

By April, the snow was melting and the Missouri River was finally free of ice. The Corps of Discovery was ready to go. Just before setting out, Captain Lewis wrote in his journal, "We were now about to penetrate a country . . . on which the foot of civilized man had never trodden."

There were thirty-three members of the expedition. Only five were not soldiers: Charbonneau, another interpreter named George Drouillard, Clark's black slave York, Sacagawea, and Pomp. They traveled in two boats called **pirogues**—one white and one red—and six smaller canoes. They launched the boats and began the hard task of traveling upstream, against the strong current of the Missouri River.

Delicious

A favorite food of the Corps of Discovery was buffalo hump. The hump, located along the bison's spine between the front shoulders, is rich in fat.

Almost immediately, Sacagawea proved her value to the expedition. She knew which plants were edible, and every day she would find and dig up roots for the soldiers to eat. It was important for them to add vegetables to their diet of buffalo and deer meat. They needed the vitamins and fiber that the roots could provide.

Fighting the current of the Missouri River was exhausting work. Sometimes the men would row the boats. Sometimes they would push with long poles stuck into the river bottom. Sometimes they would pull the boats with ropes as they walked on the riverbank. On a really good day, they could put

Sacagawea knew what plants were safe to eat, such as the bulbs of camas plants shown here.

Wild Discoveries

Lewis and Clark wrote detailed descriptions of many newly discovered animals, including the grizzly bear, prairie dog, California condor, pronghorn, and coyote. They even caught a live prairie dog to take back to Washington, D.C., for President Jefferson!

up sails and let the wind do the work. Most of the time, the corps was able to travel about 17 miles (27 kilometers) a day.

The slow progress meant that some of the men could walk along the riverbank and still keep up with the boats. Lewis and Clark decided that one of them would always stay in one of the boats but, whenever possible, the other would walk along shore. That way, they could observe any new plants or animals for their journals.

A Calm Presence

One day in May, the sails were up and the boats were cruising along. The usual boatsman took a break and gave Charbonneau control of the white pirogue. Breaking their own rule, both captains were walking along shore that day.

Suddenly, the wind became a **squall**. It pulled the sail out of Charbonneau's hands, and the pirogue tipped. This boat contained the most valuable items of the expedition— medicines, navigational instruments, the captains' journals— and the weakest swimmers, including Sacagawea and Pomp.

The only thing that kept the boat from rolling over completely was the fallen sail. Lewis and Clark shouted orders from the shore and even fired their guns in the air, but they could not be heard over the wind and the roaring river. Lewis nearly jumped into the water to swim to the boat, but at this spot the river was about 300 yards (275 meters) wide—as wide as three football fields laid end to end. He would have drowned in the rough water if he had jumped in.

The men on board finally got the boat upright, but it was almost filled with water. Delicate instruments and irreplaceable medicines were floating away. In the midst of all the panicked men, Sacagawea, with Pomp in one arm, reached out and scooped the items out of the water one by one. She caught almost everything that had washed overboard.

That night, Lewis wrote in his journal, "I cannot recollect but with the utmost **trepidation** and horror . . . the upsetting and narrow escape of the white perogue." Later, he praised Sacagawea for having "equal **fortitude** and **resolution**, with any person on board at the time of the accedent [accident]."

This painting shows Lewis and Clark aboard one of their boats before the incident.

There was no way that the expedition would survive the trip through the rapids and over the falls. The only solution was to travel around them.

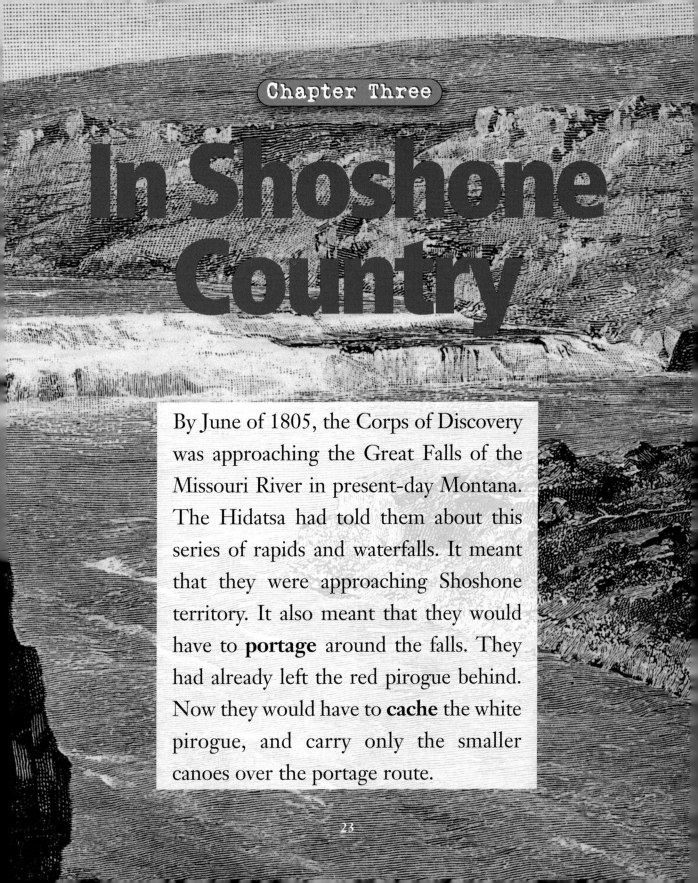

Chapter Three

In Shoshone Country

By June of 1805, the Corps of Discovery was approaching the Great Falls of the Missouri River in present-day Montana. The Hidatsa had told them about this series of rapids and waterfalls. It meant that they were approaching Shoshone territory. It also meant that they would have to **portage** around the falls. They had already left the red pirogue behind. Now they would have to **cache** the white pirogue, and carry only the smaller canoes over the portage route.

Slow Going

The Corps of Discovery took ten days to portage 18 miles (29 km). That's an average of less than 2 miles (3.2 km) a day.

Lewis took water from this mineral spring, hoping to cure Sacagawea's illness.

The Portage Is Delayed

The captains were concerned, however. Sacagawea was sick. She had a fever and pain in her abdomen. Lewis and Clark used the best treatments they knew of. They bled her, which means they cut her skin and let some of her blood run out, so that it would let some of the illness run out too. They gave her medicines to relieve her pain and to help her rest.

After almost a week, Sacagawea was not getting any better. The captains started to worry about her and about what would happen if she did not recover. They worried about the baby, Pomp, who relied on his mother's milk as his only source of food. Finally, they couldn't help worrying about themselves.

Without Sacagawea, they would not be able to communicate with the Shoshone for the horses they needed to get over the mountains. The whole expedition was in jeopardy.

Captain Lewis decided to try a different approach. While scouting for the best place to make the portage, he had seen a mineral spring. It smelled of sulfur and iron, two minerals that are important for nutrition. Captain Lewis guessed that those minerals might be what Sacagawea needed. He collected some of the water and made Sacagawea sip it slowly.

The treatment worked. The next day, Sacagawea's fever was gone and she could sit up. In a few more days she was recovered, and the portage around the Great Falls could begin.

A Familiar Place

Every day brought the Corps of Discovery closer to the mountains. One day, Sacagawea had important news for the captains. She had been here before. They were nearing the place where the Hidatsa had kidnapped her five years earlier. As they continued, she showed them the place where her family had been camped, and then the exact spot where she had been grabbed.

With that information, Lewis decided to walk ahead with three of his men to look for the Shoshone. He did not ask Sacagawea to go along. He did ask her how to say "white man"

Lewis was the first to approach the Shoshone.

in Shoshone, so that he could greet them if he found them. There was no such word in her language, however. The Shoshone had never seen a white man. Sacagawea tried to think of a good substitute word. She told him the word for "stranger."

Lewis left his interpreter behind and marched off with his guns, ready to yell "Stranger!" to the first Shoshone he met. After all, Lewis probably could only communicate with Sacagawea using sign language. If he was going to use sign language anyway, he decided he would use it directly with the Shoshone, if and when he found them.

A Family Reunion

A few days later, Clark and the rest of the expedition caught up with Lewis. Lewis had indeed found the Shoshone. He was staying in their village as the guest of the chief, Cameahwait. Together, Lewis and Cameahwait greeted Clark and the others.

Suddenly, a Shoshone woman ran forward. She recognized Sacagawea. They hugged and cried and laughed. After five years, Sacagawea was home.

Lewis and Clark were too concerned about horses to pay much attention to Sacagawea's reunion. They were also anxious to ask Cameahwait about the best route across the Rocky Mountains, now looming ahead of them. Finally, it was time for Sacagawea to interpret for the captains.

Lewis and Clark set up a translation chain. The captains

would say something in English to one of their men, Private Francois Labiche, who also spoke French. Then Labiche would repeat the phrase in French to Charbonneau. Charbonneau would say it in Hidatsa to Sacagawea. Then Sacagawea

This is the site of Camp Fortunate where Lewis and Clark met the Shoshone.

Many Nations

As they traveled across the continent, the Corps of Discovery would encounter nearly fifty different American Indian nations, including the Missouri, Yankton and Teton Sioux, Oto, Arikara, Wishram, Walla Walla, Chinook, Tillamook, and Blackfoot. Each encounter was a test of the corps' communication skills.

would say it in Shoshone to Cameahwait. When Cameahwait answered, the whole process would be reversed.

As Sacagawea started to translate, however, she stopped and looked hard at the chief. Suddenly, she jumped up and ran to him, throwing her arms around him and crying. Cameahwait was her brother. The captains had to wait for Sacagawea to stop crying before they could continue their discussion with the chief.

Negotiations

During the next few days, Lewis and Clark talked with the Shoshone leaders about getting through the mountains. Cameahwait told them that it would be very difficult, and they knew he was right. Instead of gentle peaks smaller than the Appalachians, as Jefferson had read, the Rockies consisted of one huge mountain range after another. Even now, in August, the peaks were capped with snow. Lewis and Clark were determined to get to the Pacific, however. They would cross those mountains no matter what—and they needed horses to do it.

The captains offered beads, knives, tobacco, and clothing in exchange for horses. Cameahwait, however, was a smart trader. He knew the expedition would fail without horses. His people were hungry, and winter was coming. He could trade the captains' trinkets to other tribes for food. The price of horses kept going up.

Lewis and Clark were able to buy twenty-nine horses. Still, most of the men would have to walk so that the horses could

carry supplies. The captains also hired a number of Shoshone women to carry supplies part of the way. Lewis ordered Charbonneau to buy a horse for Sacagawea and Pomp.

On the freezing morning of September 1, 1805, the Corps of Discovery set out to cross the Rocky Mountains. Sacagawea, so recently reunited with her family and friends, said goodbye to them. She was going to see the Pacific Ocean.

Sacagawea left her people to remain with the expedition.

The Rocky Mountains posed a huge obstacle for the expedition.

Chapter Four

To See the Great Waters

Crossing the Rocky Mountains was the most difficult part of the entire journey for the Corps of Discovery. There was no trail to follow. Their Shoshone guide got lost, and they had to retrace their steps over rough ridges and through steep ravines. Snow fell 8 inches (20.3 centimeters) deep on some days. They could find no large animals to hunt. Near starvation and with the end of the mountains nowhere in sight, they resorted to killing three of their smallest horses for food.

The expedition had to battle the deep snow and freezing cold weather while they crossed the Rocky Mountains.

Worst of all, they discovered there was no easy connection between the Missouri and the Columbia Rivers, as they had hoped. Instead, they found only more mountains. If they ever returned home, Lewis and Clark would have to tell President Jefferson that the Northwest Passage did not exist.

A Token of Peace

Finally, after almost three weeks in the mountains, the expedition caught sight of open plains below. They scrambled out of the mountains as fast as they could. Soon they would be heading downstream, on the way to the Pacific Ocean.

First they needed food, and they needed canoes to get down the rivers. The Shoshone had told them that the Nez Perce nation of American Indians lived on the western side of the mountains and could help them. The Nez Perce took the explorers in and fed them all the berries and dried fish they could eat. They told Lewis and Clark how to reach the Columbia River by water. They also helped the corps build canoes.

The Nez Perce noticed that the white strangers had many guns. The heavily armed expedition looked like it might be a war party. In addition, the corps were so sick and weak that the

Exhausted and starving, the members of the expedition hoped that the Nez Perce would help them after their trip through the mountains.

Nez Perce could have easily overpowered them and taken all their guns. With so many guns, the Nez Perce would become more powerful than any other American Indian nation.

The Nez Perce also noticed Sacagawea and Pomp. Reasoning that the white men would not bring a young mother and child with them if they were planning war, the Nez Perce decided that the corps had indeed come in peace. The Nez Perce did not attack the weakened members of the expedition.

Lewis and Clark realized that Sacagawea's presence had helped to protect them. They were grateful to her and to the Nez Perce for their friendship. Captain Clark wrote in his journal, "A woman with a party of men is a token of peace."

"Ocian in view!"

A few weeks later, the Corps of Discovery was heading downstream on the Columbia River. On November 7, 1805, they reached the mouth of the Columbia River. It was not yet open ocean, but the river had widened and ocean tides were flowing in, against the river current. Satisfied that they had reached the end of the continent, Captain Clark wrote, "Ocian in view! O! the joy."

The weather was terrible. It was cold, and it rained every day. They had to find a place to spend the winter, however. In their canoes, the corps explored the mouth of the Columbia and the Pacific shores nearby. The waves were high in the ocean inlets and many of the men got seasick. Finally, Lewis and Clark decided to put the matter of shelter to a vote.

Too Much Too Quickly

The starving men of the corps gorged themselves on the berries and fish. After a sparse diet of mostly meat, they were not used to these new foods. Most of them got so sick that they couldn't get up for almost a week.

Each member of the expedition, including the slave, York, and Sacagawea, cast one vote to decide the best place to build a fort. Back in the United States, this was unheard of. Blacks, most of whom were slaves, were not allowed to vote. Neither were women or American Indians. But this was the wilderness, and the Corps of Discovery had been through many hardships together. Everyone would have his or her say.

Sacagawea casts her vote, suggesting that the fort be built in an area with plenty of wapato roots.

No Ships in Sight

Lewis and Clark spent the winter watching for ships on the ocean. They were hoping to send news of their success (and safety) by ship back to President Jefferson. They never did see a ship.

35

Once again, Sacagawea showed her good sense. She voted for a place where they could find **wapato** roots, which the Nez Perce harvested for food. Using Sacagawea's nickname, Clark recorded her vote with all the rest: "Janey in favour of a place where there is plenty of Potas [wapatos]."

The Corps of Discovery built Fort Clatsop, named after a tribe of American Indians living in the area. Then they settled in for the winter. Deep snows in the Rocky Mountains would make it impossible to cross back again until spring. The captains spent the winter exploring the area and making detailed maps. They wrote down everything they could about the people, plants, and animals they encountered on the Pacific coast. It rained almost every day.

A Bold Request

Shortly after New Year's Day in 1806, the corps heard exciting news. A whale had washed ashore a few miles away. The captains were very excited for the chance to see such an animal up close and to record their findings.

Lewis and Clark prepared for the hike to see the whale. They chose a few men to go with them so they could bring back meat and blubber for everyone. As they were getting ready to go, Sacagawea stood up. She had something to say. Captain Lewis recorded it in his journal:

"She observed that she had traveled a long way with us to see the great waters, and that now that monstrous fish was also to be seen, she thought it very hard she could not be permitted to see either." The captains could not argue with that. They let Sacagawea come along to see the whale.

Sacagawea takes a moment to enjoy the Pacific Ocean, a site she had traveled so far to see.

In their notes and journals, Lewis and Clark wrote about people, animals, plants, and places they encountered on their journey. When they returned, they would tell the world about their many discoveries.

Chapter Five

Homeward

Lewis and Clark had reached their goal. They had traveled the entire distance from the Mississippi River to the Pacific Ocean and had made new discoveries almost every day. Now they couldn't wait to start their journey homeward.

In late March of 1806, the Corps of Discovery left Fort Clatsop and headed back east, up the Columbia River. The captains decided they would spend a few weeks with their friends, the Nez Perce, at the foot of the Rocky Mountains. Then, as soon as the snow was melting, they would be ready to start their trek through the mountains.

Back Among Friends

Once again, the Nez Perce welcomed the corps and fed them. The Indians had kept the expedition's horses for them over the winter and would sell them more. They provided five guides to help Lewis and Clark get back through the mountains.

The guides led the corps expertly through the mountains. The passage that had taken eleven days the previous fall took only six days now. The guides were so skilled that they could follow the trail even though much of it was still covered with snow.

Safely back on the east side of the Rockies, Lewis and Clark parted ways for the only time during the journey. They wanted to explore different routes on their way back to the Mandan villages. Sacagawea, Pomp, and Charbonneau went with Clark's group overland to the Yellowstone River. Then they would go by canoe to the Missouri, where they hoped to meet up with Lewis's group for the trip to the Mandan villages.

Sacagawea was back in Shoshone lands. However, she never did return to the village of her brother, Cameahwait. Captain Clark wanted to go back a different way. Sacagawea missed her chance to stay with her people. There is no mention in Clark's journal that she protested. The whale incident proves that Sacagawea wasn't afraid to speak up to the captains and to make her wishes known. One can only guess that she decided she belonged with Charbonneau and the Mandan Indians on the plains.

Touching the Sky

Lewis and Clark had once envisioned the Rocky Mountains to be smaller than the 6,500-foot (1,980-m) peaks of the Appalachians. In fact, the range of the Rockies where they crossed, known as the Bitterroots, had peaks that were nearly 11,000 feet (3,353 m) high—almost twice as high as they had expected.

A Source of Guidance

One day, the trail opened onto two different mountain passes. Captain Clark had never been here before. He tried to decide which pass led to the Yellowstone River. The area was familiar to Sacagawea, however. She knew which way to go. According to Captain Clark, "The indian woman who has been of great service to me as a pilot through this country recommends a gap in the mountain more south, which I shall cross." It was the second time during the journey that Sacagawea acted as a guide for the captains.

As they approached the Yellowstone River, Clark's party

When the expedition split up, Sacagawea traveled with Clark to the Yellowstone River.

Twice during the expedition, Sacagawea was able to help the expedition find their way.

came upon a large, flat **outcropping** of rock rising from the plains. They found carvings in the sandstone that were left by earlier generations of American Indians. Clark carved his own name and the date into the rock and named it Pompy's Tower, after Sacagawea's son.

Finally, in August 1806, Captain Clark's group reached the Missouri River, where they rejoined Captain Lewis's group for the trip down the river to the Mandan village. They arrived at the Mandan village on August 14, 1806—one year and four months after starting out.

Lewis and Clark prepared for the last leg of their journey down the Missouri and Mississippi Rivers to St. Louis. Captain Clark offered to take Pomp back to St. Louis to give him an education. Sacagawea told him that Pomp was not yet old enough, but in one year she would allow him to go. The captains paid Charbonneau for his services to

A Look at History

Pompy's Tower is the only place along the entire route where visitors can see clear evidence of Lewis and Clark's journey. Visitors can see Clark's carving in the rock: "Wm. Clark July 25, 1806." Now called Pompey's Pillar National Monument, it is about 30 miles (48 km) east of Billings, Montana, and it is open to the public.

This map shows the routes taken by the Corps of Discovery.

The expedition traveled thousands of miles before the end of their journey.

the Corps of Discovery in the amount of $500.33. That amount is equivalent to approximately $5,800 today—still not much money for sixteen months of work. Sacagawea was paid nothing.

On August 17, 1806, Lewis and Clark left the Mandan village for St. Louis, where they would receive a huge welcome as national heroes. Sacagawea went back to her quiet life on the plains.

An Unexpected Return

After the corps had been gone for more than two years, no one really expected to see Lewis and Clark again. They were greeted with huge celebrations when they returned home.

An Offer of Thanks

Heading downstream, Captain Clark had time to think about the service and sacrifice of Sacagawea. He wrote a letter to Charbonneau. It contained his typical creative spellings, and once again Clark used Sacagawea's nickname, Janey:

"Your woman who accompanied you that long dangerous and fatigueing rout to the Pacific Ocian and back, diserved a greater reward for her attention and Services on that rout than we had in our power to give her at the Mandans. As to your little Son (my boy Pomp) you well know my fondness for him. . . . I once more tell you if you will bring your son . . . to me, I will educate him and treat him as my own child.

"Charbono, . . . if you . . . will bring down your Son . . . Janey had best come along with you to take care of the boy untill I get him."

Charbonneau would accept Captain Clark's offer three years later.

President Thomas Jefferson was thrilled to learn about all of the discoveries made by the Lewis and Clark expedition.

Chapter Six

A Remarkable Life

Back in Washington, D.C., President Jefferson was delighted with the accomplishments of the Corps of Discovery. Despite the disappointing news that there was no Northwest Passage, the expedition was a huge success. Lewis and Clark were heroes. Congress awarded every member of the expedition double pay and a grant of 320 acres (130 hectares) of land.

When Charbonneau heard about the money and land coming to him, he decided it was time to accept Clark's offer and go to St. Louis. He took Sacagawea and four-year-old Pomp with him. It was the fall of 1809.

Charbonneau stayed less than two years. In March of 1811, he sold his land to Captain Clark for $100 and joined an expedition going up the Missouri River to establish a fur-trading post. There was a man named Henry Brackenridge on board the boat going upriver. He wrote about traveling with Charbonneau and Sacagawea, "both of whom accompanied Lewis and Clark to the Pacific, and were of great service." Brackenridge did not mention a little boy with them. Pomp had stayed in St. Louis to be educated by Captain Clark, just as was promised.

A Disputed Ending

The fur traders built Fort Manuel along the Missouri River in what is now South Dakota. Sacagawea stayed there while Charbonneau left for long months to go trapping. The fort's clerk, John Luttig, kept a daily journal of activities in the fort. In August 1812, he wrote that Sacagawea gave birth to a daughter and named her Lisette. Then, on December 20, he wrote this about Sacagawea:

"This Evening the wife of Charbonneau, a Snake Squaw, died of a putrid fever she was a good and the best woman in the fort, aged about 25 years she left a fine infant girl."

By the following spring, the War of 1812 had extended to the Missouri River. Fort Manuel was attacked and burned

down by Indians fighting for the British. The fort had to be abandoned. No one knew what had happened to Toussaint Charbonneau.

Luttig knew that Clark was already caring for Sacagawea's son, Pomp, in St. Louis. In the summer of 1813, Luttig took Lisette to St. Louis to join them. Now that their mother was dead and their father had disappeared, Clark went to court and signed papers making him the legal guardian of both Lisette and Pomp. A few years later, Clark made a list of *Men on Lewis and Clarks Trip*, noting the whereabouts of each

It was reported that Sacagawea died at Fort Manuel in 1812.

William Clark looked after Charbonneau and Sacagawea's children and served as their guardian.

member of the expedition. After Sacagawea's name, he wrote simply, "Dead."

This was a sad and early end to an extraordinary life, yet new stories about Sacagawea persisted. More than forty years later, sometime in the 1850s, an old woman arrived on the Wind River Shoshone reservation in Wyoming and claimed to be Sacagawea. She told stories no one else could tell—stories of near-starvation in the mountains, and of seeing the great ocean and the great fish. She lived until 1884. If she really was Sacagawea, she would have been almost one hundred years old.

Pomp's Adventures

When Pomp was eighteen years old, he met a visiting German prince and traveled with him to Europe. He studied and traveled there for six years. Pomp then returned to the United States and became a respected wilderness guide.

It may never be known for certain which story is true. The second account is certainly a much better story and a happier ending. However, most evidence points to the conclusion that Sacagawea died young at Fort Manuel in the winter of 1812. Clark was educating and caring for her son, Pomp. Most likely, Clark kept in touch with Sacagawea and always knew of her whereabouts. It is unlikely he would adopt Sacagawea's daughter if she were still living.

A Remarkable Life

No matter which story is true, Sacagawea's contributions to Lewis and Clark's expedition across the West were important. She traveled thousands of miles, to the Pacific Ocean and back, while caring for a baby. She helped to find food, acted as interpreter, and was a symbol of peace. She endured bitter cold, blistering heat, gnawing hunger, and feverish illness without complaint.

Sacagawea was an American Indian among white soldiers. She was a young girl among thirty-one men, yet she spoke her mind and earned the respect of each member of the expedition. Eventually, President Jefferson read the

Sacagawea will always be remembered for the crucial role she played in the Lewis and Clark expedition.

Dollar Coin

Sacagawea is commemorated on the gold-colored one-dollar coin, which went into circulation in January 2000.

bits and pieces that Lewis and Clark had written about Sacagawea in their journals. It is not known if he put the pieces together in his mind to gain an impression of Sacagawea and her contribution to the expedition. It is also not known if Jefferson realized that without her the expedition might have failed. Still, he had something in common with this Shoshone Indian girl. They both played a part in making Jefferson's grand vision a reality. The United States would become a large and powerful nation.

Sacagawea's life has become legend. Some people have given her credit for guiding the entire expedition single-handedly through the wilderness, fearlessly pointing the way for the white men. Some people say that, later, she wandered the West alone for years, finally returning home to her Shoshone people. Some people say that she was nothing more than a young girl, swept along by others into history. The truth is somewhere in between. No matter where the truth lies, Sacagawea's life was truly remarkable.

Timeline

1789?   Sacagawea is born in a northern Shoshone village in present-day Idaho.

1800   Sacagawea is captured by Hidatsa raiders. She is about eleven years old.

1801   Thomas Jefferson becomes president of the United States.

1804   Lewis and Clark build Fort Mandan late in the year. They ask Charbonneau and Sacagawea to join the Corps of Discovery as interpreters.

1805   Sacagawea gives birth to Jean Baptiste on February 11. The Corps of Discovery sets out up the Missouri River on April 7. Sacagawea is reunited with her Shoshone people in August. She helps Lewis and Clark negotiate for horses.

1806   In January, Sacagawea walks with Lewis and Clark to see the beached whale. She returns to the Mandan village in August. Charbonneau is paid $500.33, but Sacagawea is paid nothing. Clark offers to take her son with him to St. Louis for an education.

1809   Charbonneau, Sacagawea, and Pomp travel to St. Louis to claim their land grant.

1811   Charbonneau and Sacagawea return to the Missouri River, leaving Pomp with Clark.

1812   At Fort Manuel in present-day South Dakota, Sacagawea gives birth to a daughter, Lisette, in August. Sacagawea dies of "a putrid fever" at Fort Manuel on December 20. She is about twenty-five years old.

1884   A Shoshone woman claiming to be Sacagawea dies on the Wind River Indian Reservation in Wyoming. She is about one hundred years old.

Glossary

ambition—strong desire to achieve a goal

cache—to hide provisions or implements for later use

coincidence—two things happening at the same time by accident

commission—an official granting of military rank

corps—an organized military group; a group of people working together to perform one job

fortitude—courage

native—originating in a particular place

negotiate—to talk with another person in order to arrive at an agreement; to discuss a fair trade

outcropping—a rock that rises above the surrounding ground

pirogue—a large, flat-bottomed riverboat

portage—to carry goods overland from one body of water to another or around an obstacle

resolution—determination

squall—a sudden violent wind

trepidation—fear

wapato—an edible root

To Find Out More

Books

Alter, Judy. *Exploring and Mapping the American West*. Danbury, Conn.: Children's Press, 2001.

Davis, Lucile. *Medicine in the American West*. Danbury, Conn.: Children's Press, 2001.

Hunsaker, Joyce Badgley. *Sacagawea Speaks: Beyond the Shining Mountains with Lewis and Clark*. Guilford, Conn.: TwoDot Press, 2001.

Lourie, Peter. *On the Trail of Sacagawea*. Honesdale, Penn.: Boyds Mills Press, 2001.

Santella, Andrew. *Lewis and Clark*. Danbury, Conn.: Franklin Watts, 2001.

St. George, Judith. *Sacagawea*. New York: Philomel Books, 1997.

Webster, Christine. *The Lewis and Clark Expedition*. Danbury, Conn.: Children's Press, 2003.

Video

Lewis and Clark: The Journey of the Corps of Discovery. Florentine Films/WETA, 1997.

Organizations and Online Sites

Lewis and Clark: The Journey of the Corps of Discovery
http://www.pbs.org/lewisandclark
This is the companion site to the documentary on the expedition done by Ken Burns. The site provides interactive stories about the journey.

The Lewis and Clark Journey of Discovery
http://www.nps.gov/jeff/
Created by the National Park Service, this site offers a brief and accurate summary of Sacagawea's life.

Montana Historical Society
225 N. Roberts
P. O. Box 201201
Helena, MT 59620-1201
http://www.discoveringmontana.com/MHSweb/lewisandclark/css/default.asp
This organization sponsors a museum and research library. Its site provides accounts of the expedition in Montana, including an "Ask the Librarian" page where students can e-mail questions about the expedition in Montana.

New Perspectives on the West: Sacagawea
http://www.pbs.org/weta/thewest/people/s_z/sacagawea.htm
A companion site to a Public Broadcasting Service documentary on the West, this site has a short biography of Sacagawea.

Pompey's Pillar National Monument
http://www.mt.blm.gov/pillarmon/index.html
Run by the Montana Bureau of Land Management, this site provides information on visiting this monument.

A Note on Sources

Everything we know about Sacagawea's life is written in the journals and letters of Meriwether Lewis, William Clark, and a few others during a very short period of her life. Through their words, we catch a glimpse of a strong, brave, intelligent person who earned their respect.

The information in this book is based primarily on the words written by those people who knew Sacagawea directly: Captains Lewis and Clark, Sergeants John Ordway and Patrick Gass of the Corps of Discovery, Henry Brackenridge on the 1811 journey upriver, and John Luttig at Fort Manuel. The spelling *Sacagawea* is used in this book because it comes closest to the spelling that the journal writers used most often.

Excellent information was provided in *Undaunted Courage* by Stephen E. Ambrose, *Lewis and Clark Among the Indians* by James P. Ronda, and *Sacajawea* by Harold P. Howard. The most convincing source of information on Sacagawea's later life was Irving W. Anderson's "Probing the Riddle of the Bird Woman," published in the autumn 1973 issue of *Montana The Magazine of Western History*.

—*Stacy DeKeyser*

Index

Numbers in *italics* indicate illustrations.

About the Author

Stacy DeKeyser has always loved history. She and her family enjoy exploring historic sites—searching for wagon ruts on the Oregon Trail in Wyoming, walking along Hadrian's Wall in England, or reading gravestones in the colonial cemeteries near their Connecticut home. She is looking forward to visiting sites along the trail of the Lewis and Clark expedition. DeKeyser holds a bachelor's degree from University of California at Los Angeles and a master's degree from Arizona State University. She has published articles in numerous newspapers and magazines, and she speaks at conferences about the craft of writing.